Prai

"I have worked wi
coached hundreds   .e
of the reasons we've asked John to travel half way across the country
so many times over the years - aside from the fact that he's one of the
best in the business - is that he always provides something extra, at
no extra cost, wisdom. Read this book and you'll discover what I
mean. ... There is no question that what John really does for a living
is help others succeed. 'Lessons From The Field' is only the most
recent evidence of that. It won't take you long to read it - the lessons
truly are, after all, simple - but I'm confident that the few hours you
spend reading it will be one of the best investments you could make
of your time."

- Wendell Potter, Vice President, Corporate and Executive Communications, CIGNA
Corporation

"May God bless this book and soften the hearts and call to action
those who read it. ... A heart felt, straightforward message about life
from a guy who works with business people that are sometimes too
busy to be bothered with life. ... I have been blessed though his simple
yet profound questions to grow as a husband, father, friend and CEO.
If you aspire to lead, learn these lessons from John's farm."

- James Sharman, President & CEO, World Kitchen, Inc.

"John Brekke brings both calm and urgency to the essential elements
of living a balanced life. In this short volume, he combines practical
advice with personal stories illustrating the impact of his approach.
Essential advice for leaders and those aspiring to be leaders."

- Matthew Rampton, Head of Business Development, BT Americas, Inc.

"The advice in this book is sound advice... I am a much better person
and executive because of working with John. Read the book apply the
wisdom and you too shall reap the benefits."

- Clint Larson, Corporate Vice President, Honeywell, Inc. (Retired)

"John's ability to help executives grow is reflected in this 'Lessons
From The Field,' which yields a cornucopia of practical ideas for the
reader to harvest."

- Charlie Graves, CEO, Conner Sport Court

"Lessons from the Field" is an excellent, quick read for aspiring or established leaders of organizations reminding all of us of the importance of balance in our lives.

- Donald H. Hofreuter, MD, Administrator / COO, Wheeling Hospital

"...I loved the stories about the people who discovered the secret of life balance. The fifty year old successful manager who began to share his experiences regarding his five year old brought a tear to my eye. It is truly a joyful thing to see already successful people who go from being effective managers, to being even better leaders who will leave a legacy of inspired and dedicated employees."

- Bill Werner, Vice President & General Manager, Motorola Inc.

"In a world where 'Leadership' has become a science, analyzed and dissected in countless books, articles, and speeches, John Brekke's 'Lessons from the Field' provides a refreshing change of pace. Rather than taking the reader through academic prose, charts, outlines, and footnotes to prove various leadership theories, Brekke instead asks us to consider a few, common sense lessons. Setting priorities, leading integrated and balanced lives, recognizing our obligations to others - these are what lead to a lasting legacy, the true definition of leadership. Brekke's book provides much wisdom in a small package."

- Larry W. Stranghoener, Executive Vice President & Chief Financial Officer, The Mosaic Company

"The analogies you drew to the different phases of farming help make, and I believe will help keep, the message crystal clear - long after the reader has put down the book."

- Jenette E. Fetzner, Vice-President, National Accounts, CIGNA Healthcare

LESSONS FROM THE FIELD

LESSONS FROM THE FIELD

SIMPLE LESSONS ABOUT SUCCESS, LEADERSHIP
AND LIVING A BALANCED LIFE

JOHN L. BREKKE
& DAVID L. BREKKE

CONTENTS

WITH ADMIRATION I DEDICATE THIS BOOK TO...

John Bucksbaum, CEO General Growth Properties, Inc., who with his wife Jackie, is seeking to "live it right."

George Norman, (Uncle George) who years after his passing is still teaching me how to farm.

And all the many unnamed business professionals mentioned in this book. Most business-oriented books use the names of companies and individuals with the stories that are told. I've chosen not to. I'm convinced that the value of these stories is self evident, and that knowing the notoriety or obscurity of the people mentioned would simply be distracting. But I do not wish the individuals to go unrecognized...

So to all the great leaders and companies I've had the pleasure of working with these last two decades I doff my hat. Thank you. It has been an honor...

INTRODUCTION

I became an executive coach years before it was fashionable. A lucky break led me to a grant from the Kellogg Foundation to study leadership inside corporations, and I've been a student of leadership ever since. I've spent a great many hours in boardrooms coaching individual CEOs and executive teams since 1979. It's been a remarkable journey. For more than 20 years I've worked with Kellogg Foundation grant recipients in their groundbreaking studies, and in my own work as a coach for some of the best and brightest CEOs in the U.S.

Despite years of training and experience as an executive coach in the corporate sector, I am still a farmer at heart.

I spent my early years in northern Minnesota, the product of a farming community. My earliest lessons were at the feet of my Uncle George, who ran the family farm with a tenacious spirit and great love for the land.

For many years I have owned a small farm in rural Minnesota, where digging in the dirt keeps me rooted in what's important. After a draining session with a top executive team, I travel back to my little patch of dirt, where I plow, weed, water, and savor the miracles that occur every year.

In this book I am going to invite you out to my farm. Not a vast, flat modern farm, but a small, hilly farm in the woods of rural Minnesota. Here you will put on a hat and overalls I will loan to you and ride my '46 Ford tractor. You will hoe, water, weed, and here, as my guest, you will learn about farming, and about leadership, and about life.

What we are growing this year is people, and what we are harvesting is nothing less than your legacy. You know that you can be greater than what you have been. So don your hat and grab a hoe. It's time to break some ground.

PLOWING STRAIGHT

"No one who puts his hand to the plow and looks back
is fit for service in the kingdom of God."

Luke 9:62 NIV

Recently, I brought one of my CEO clients to my
farm in Minnesota for a long weekend. His is a name
you'd recognize, his influence vast and his organization
enormous. But on this day in Minnesota, he was wearing
an old pair of overalls I'd loaned him, and we were
discussing the fine art of plowing with a tractor.

He was eager to try. I instructed him, "Never look
back from where you've come when you're plowing your
first furrow – always keep your vision focused on the
fence post ahead of you. This ensures you will plow a
straight furrow. That first straight furrow is imperative
because it sets up the field for straight plowing. In fact,
after you've created a straight furrow up and back, the
tractor will practically drive itself because the tires will
have this straight furrow as a guide.

He climbed aboard the tractor and began plowing. His smile was broad, he was confident of his ability to do the job and do it well. He waved to me, wiping his brow in the hot sun as he continued. By now he'd plowed half the length of the field. But he couldn't resist: he looked back over his shoulder to admire his work. But what he didn't realize is that every time he turned to look, the wheel of the tractor moved *ever so slightly*. The rows became more and more crooked, and when he realized his mistake, he stopped. Apologizing profusely, he said he'd fix the problem and get it right this time.

What should have taken an hour, took him all afternoon.

"Did you learn the lesson?" I asked when he finished, and he nodded.

It was one of my better coaching moments, where the lessons I'd learned on the farm were one and the same with my work with senior executives: If you want to plow straight, to "set up" your field, you have to focus on your future, your goal – not your past.

WHAT IS SUCCESS?

Everyone wants to be successful; few people know what that means. "Success" is simply the state of having accomplished a goal. There are a plethora of books out there that can help you define and achieve a goal. For most people, however, the term "success" means far more. Being "successful," having "arrived," having "made it," is achieving the goal of being where you want to be in the larger scheme of life. This goal is something akin to Abraham Maslow's "self-actualization" or "self-transcendence" category,[1] or Viktor Frankl's "will to meaning" concept,[2] but the point can be conveyed most clearly by the outcome, happiness. Everyone wants to be successful, few people know what they are actually searching for is happiness, and fewer still, know how to achieve it.

It reminds me of an old joke: One farmer says to another, "Don't you love the way the rich dirt feels in your hands? The smell of rain on the new sprouts? The

---

[1] Abraham Maslow, Toward a Psychology of Being, 2nd Edition (New York: Van Nostrand, 1968) and The Further Reaches of Human Nature (New York: Penguin, 1971).
[2] Viktor Frankl, Man's Search for Meaning (New York: Washington Square Press, 1963).

sound of wind on a golden field of wheat?" The other farmer shrugs, "Eh, I'm in it for the money."

I have found that the idea of farming almost universally appeals to people on at least some level. Why is that? I think it has to do with the way of life people imagine when they think of farming. For some people farming represents simplicity and quiet, for others vitality and health, and for others life long friends and strong family bonds.

What does it mean to be a successful farmer? More money? More power? More prestige? Hardly. Anyone who likes the idea of farming for these reasons has been sadly misinformed. And yet, time and time again, when I tell people about my little farm they get this far off wistful look, "Yeah, that would be nice."

A CEO I work with has lots of toys and other trappings of success – easily measurable yardsticks of success. His last two cars were together worth more than $250,000, and he owns a plane and multiple houses. But if asked to define his success, he speaks in terms of people, not things. With love and pride, he talks about his kids and his wife of 35 years, and he mentions the people he's had the opportunity to connect with. Success for him is measured as a whole life experience.

By contrast, I talked with a guy last year that was a senior vice president in a company that endured a divestiture. He went to another company, again as a senior vice president. Three months later his part of the business was sold to a competitor; a replication of authority put him out of a job again. All this happened within a year. We were talking on the phone and I asked him, "How are you dealing with all this?"

"Last week," he said, "I didn't think I was going to make it. I've really been depressed. It's not the money; the company set me up with a nice severance package," he said, "but I'm just realizing that I measure my worth by my career – period. My wife and I are fighting, the kids are seeing Dad at home all day not doing what he wants to be doing, and I was thinking that I should just cash it in."

"Are you talking suicide?" I asked.

"Well, there are worse things. My wife would get along fine without me."

This is a dramatic example of someone whose narrow definition of success could have cost him his life. Fortunately, he sought counseling to help him through his crisis. His story can help us all face the question: how do we define ourselves? If your worth is solely based on your career, you risk losing yourself if you lose your job. Step back from your present situation and consider the benefits of adjusting a few ideas and attitudes. Can you "have it all?" Yes. But first you need to define what "having it all" means.

The executives who inspired this book know success is measured differently. They see success in terms of a family who loves and cares for them, good health, devoted friends and as a continual process of helping others throughout their lives. They realized that business success is an outgrowth of other successful components – and hopefully so will you.

I'm often asked what the secret of success is. After more than 20 years of observing some of the most accomplished business leaders in the nation, I've boiled down success to three essentials areas: Setting life priorities. Helping others succeed. Having a sense of urgency. In this chapter we will look at the first of these three.

THE 1ST KEY TO SUCCESS: SETTING LIFE PRIORITIES

Years ago I was asked by a multinational company to make a presentation on the first night of a three-day management committee retreat. It was a presentation I've given for a number of years called "Prophecy and Purpose." Presiding over the forum was the chairman and CEO, whom I had known in another company prior to his recent appointment and who was new in his position, and 30 people who ran the businesses around the world. This was his first time meeting with his new team. During the question and answer session following my presentation, someone asked me, "What do you see as priorities in the lives of the successful leaders you work with?"

I named the priorities in order, from greatest importance to least: self, family, others, work. The reaction that followed was a storm of disagreement.

"We don't buy that. That's not part of our culture here!" they said.

The discussion became heated, with me as the object of antipathy. Even so, the chairman asked me if I would stay for the next day. He said, "I'd like to change our focus for the meetings so we can get at this."

The chairman expressed concern over those who seemed to be quite productive but were clearly on the edge of burnout. We spent time creating a new meeting outline to address their corporate culture.

In our first group session the next morning, I asked people to tell me how many hours per week they worked. The average was 72.

Then, I met with them individually, and learned more about their lives. Many people talked about major health issues. They talked about family and spousal issues, failed marriages and current marriages on the rocks. They talked about children who didn't really know them.

One man's oldest child didn't want anything to do with him. The child said, "Dad, you weren't there when I needed you and now you're trying to come back into my life and buy my affection. And what I needed from you, you never, ever gave to me."

Over the next two years, I worked with the company's senior leadership to help them address life and business priorities. Two years later, when this same management team met again, we polled the group and found the average number of hours worked per week had dropped to 52. The company's bottom line had improved from where it was two years prior. Wall Street was recognizing them as a solid well run, growing company. People were healthier and more productive. They were in relationships that were more fulfilling. Many were learning what it meant to be a parent or grandparent. Simply put, they were living life more fully.

People who had re-ordered their life priorities were now able to concentrate on work without being distracted by the debris in their lives.

Stop. Once again...

People who had re-ordered their *life priorities* were now able to concentrate on *work* without being distracted by the debris in their lives. By making their work a lower priority the quality and consistency of their work improved.

PRIORITY ONE: SELF

There are three common incorrect responses to hearing that "Self" is the first priority. Practical objection: Our company (or family) couldn't survive without employees who put company objectives first. Moral objection: Selfishness is wrong; "self" should be the last priority. Hedonistic: Great! I'm gonna buy another boat with little Timmy's college fund! Each of these incorrect responses can be answered with one clarification. By "self" I do not mean self-centeredness but self-sustenance.

What is self-sustenance? Self-sustenance is fulfilling your basic needs. It is taking care of yourself in the manner encouraged by most parents. On the most basic level this means caring for your health: Look both ways before you cross the street. It's a nice day, you should get outside. Get plenty of rest. Don't get your lunch from the vending machine. Take your pills. Drink lots of water. Drive safely.

It is surprising how many people still don't understand that when you are sick you need rest and should stay home from work. Everyone at the office will likely be more productive without your grumpy, sniffly self there to bring them down and possibly make them sick too.

If you are like most people you don't need to be reminded that exercise and eating right are essential to keeping your body running. If you are like most people, however, you also don't practice either on a routine basis.

Many of my clients began diligent exercise programs at the time they were promoted into senior management positions. When asked why, they said they could see the difference the promotion would make in their lifestyle and wanted to be physically able to meet the demands of the job and enjoy the fruits of their labor. The priority of physical health wasn't self-evident earlier because of the twin truisms of rising managers: they're too busy building a career and starting a family. The good health we enjoyed as 20 year-olds lulls us into complacency until we notice a decline in our thirties and forties.

Medical science has shown that a person in good physical shape has increased physical stamina, enhanced mental capacity and greater emotional stability.

Two last things need to be said about caring for your health:

æ While everything you do by way of eating right and exercising is beneficial, in order to truly reap rewards it needs to be consistent. You can't cram for your annual physical like it was a college exam.

א Stress is like poison to your body. It is hard to find a health magazine these days that doesn't mention stress, the effect of stress on the body, or ways to alleviate stress. Stress is a legitimate health issue. Which brings us to the less obvious matters of caring for yourself.

Self-sustenance also means caring for your psyche, or soul. The executives I've worked with all have endured the cyclical nature of business and have had to deal with the accompanying emotional turmoil during quarterly losses, layoffs, restructuring and downsizing. And like many others, they've been challenged with personal life crises, too. They have learned that the nurturing of our emotional well-being can act as a foundation for our emotional responses, enhancing our ability to find strength within ourselves. The result is one of the hallmarks of good leadership: Composure during crisis.

This emotional foundation has three elements: Relate. Relax. Play.

א Relate: Humans are creatures that (while they can exist alone for extended periods of time) cannot thrive in isolation. Effective social interaction involves skills; developing those skills dramatically increases our value in the marketplace. Beyond the mercenary socializing to increase sales, to promote people and ideas, or to play office politics, the ability to interact on a meaningful level with other human beings improves our own humanity and ability to lead.

The act of dropping the facade for real interpersonal exchange can shed insight into the choices and actions of those we deal with. This is often difficult because we feel we may lose composure and control. In fact, we gain recognition as a real person and a real leader. Relating, then, is not only necessary for mental health, it helps us develop as leaders.

  ➷ Relaxation: Relaxation means very different things for different people. While extroverts often associate relaxation with social get-togethers, introverts more often find relaxation in solitude. For some it means reading the newspaper, or a book. For others, doing yoga, a hobby, or phoning an old friend. If stress is poison, relaxation is the antidote; relaxation is the antithesis of stress. Being able to relax and let go of stress is a skill, which, when developed, allows us to think clearly and act reasonably even under intense pressure.

      Recreation or play: I am using recreation in one particular way; by recreation I mean having fun. Often people confuse relaxing and having fun. Having fun is usually (but not necessarily) social. It often involves laughter, and can happen anytime without warning. I am reminded of the day I discovered that I could pop balloons from over five feet away with a toothpick stuck in a grape.

Most executives have little trouble understanding the need for a healthy lifestyle, relaxation or time socializing with others, but play can be a hang up. Play is for kids, isn't it?

One of the central concepts in the business bestseller, "Fish! *A remarkable way to boost morale and improve results"* is play. "We sell a lot of fish. We have low turnover. We enjoy work that can be very tedious. We have become great friends, like the players on a winning team. We have a lot of pride in what we do and the way we do it. And we have become world famous. [...] We know how to play!"[3]

The award winning design firm IDEO furnished its offices with large foam blocks. Originally introduced as sound dampeners they quickly became toys. The people at IDEO discovered that a fun and creative environment leads to creative ideas.[4]

It might sound frivolous but play is integral not only to being emotionally healthy, but to being a good leader.

PRIORITY TWO: FAMILY [5]

Many people like to say, "My first priority is my family. That's why I work so hard, so I can provide for the people most important to me." Unfortunately, a statement like that is oftentimes masking another more serious issue.

---

[3] Stephen Lundin, Harry Paul, John Christiansen, Fish! *A remarkable way to boost morale and improve results* (New York: Hyperion 2000).
[4] Tom Kelly, The Art of Innovation (New York: Currency Books 2001) pp. 126-128.
[5] I do not wish to ignore the fact that many choose not to marry, or are not now married. Additionally, many couples are childless. The fact remains that we are all in "families" of one sort, be it the conventional family or a family made up of extended relatives and friends.

The reality is, when you get into incisive conversations with people who work all the time "to provide for their families" you hear about a lot of disappointment in their relationships. Bad marriages, disappointed children and distanced friends. In many cases, parents and kids just don't know each other very well. Kids say, "Mom's never home." Or, "Sure, we live in a beautiful house, I got a car for my birthday, we take vacations, I can get whatever I want... but Dad just isn't around."

Elliot Weiner, in his book, The Ostrich Complex, describes this "head-in-the-sand" behavior: "The state or condition of ignoring, avoiding, or pretending that something doesn't exist with the hope that the something, usually a problem, will just go away."[6]

Long hours at the office can be our "ostrich." We can avoid the sticky issues at home while telling ourselves that we are being responsible and giving to our family by spending more time at work.

---

[6] Elliot Weiner, The Ostrich Complex (New York: Warner Books, 1986), p. 1.

But what, you may ask, does my family need from me? An exhaustive coverage of family needs is beyond the scope of this book, but allow me three suggestions:

∾ Ask. ESP withstanding, you don't know what the members of your family are hoping for in their relationship with you. It sounds simple... it is, just ask.

∾ Use a mediator. In its most sedate form a mediator is a common set of terms by which to communicate. This is easily achieved by reading a book together. An excellent book for this purpose is, "The Five Love Languages" by Gary Chapman. Chapman argues that there are five primary ways in which people communicate love. When two people's love language doesn't match (which is usually the case) their attempts to show love to the other person are not received to the extent that they are given.[7] A more active form of mediation is counseling. A good counselor acts as a translator, helping people understand the very human needs that underlie each other's often painful and confusing behavior.

---

[7] Gary Chapman, The Five Love Languages: How to express heartfelt commitment to your mate (Northfield Publishers 1992). See also, The Five Love Languages of Children (Northfield Publishers 1997).

❧ Consecrate time for them. The greatest gift you can give is consecrated time. Consecrated time is time during which your attention is focused on one thing, in this case, your family. Not only does it require you to not be doing anything else, it also requires you to not be thinking about anything else. Giving away consecrated time is a skill that can be developed like any other... with practice.

PRIORITY THREE: COMMUNITY

One of my clients has a best friend he's been close to since they were together in the military. Over the years, through illnesses and family crises, he has always said, "If my friend needs me, I'll do whatever is necessary to be with him." He stayed with him through the good times - graduation, wedding, birth of children - and the bad times alcoholism, job loss, death of a child.

That friendship created an anchor of stability in the lives of these two men. My client's reward is the incredible loyalty the bond nurtured. In return for the support he gave, he could expect a shoulder to lean on when things would occasionally disintegrate in his own life.

Besides a close friend, many people regularly get together with a group of friends who share common interests, such as hunting, sports, music and other hobbies. Others devote personal time with formally organized groups who share a common cause - from politics to the environment, or one of the many service organizations.

Other people belong to a spiritual community. The church is important to them not just because of the religious teachings, but also because of the community of people who are part of that church. It's the sense of community that sustains them.

Whatever your form of community, remember this one truism: What you get out of your relationships is directly proportional to what you put into them.

PRIORITY FOUR: WORK

Those who say, "Work absolutely comes first!" aren't usually as productive, efficient and happy as the person who says, "Work is important, but other things are even more important." What I keep hearing from leaders is that if you have these kinds of priorities in order, it means that when you come to work you can concentrate on the work, and you are therefore more productive.

Peter Drucker, one of America's foremost business thinkers says, "If there is any one 'secret' of effectiveness, it is concentration. Effective executives do first things first and they do one thing at a time."[8]

"Concentration - that is, the courage to impose on time and events his own decision as to what really matters and comes first - is the executive's only hope of becoming the master of time and events instead of their whipping boy."[9]

---

[8] Peter F. Drucker, The Effective Executive (New York: HarperBusiness, 1967), p. 100.
[9] Peter F. Drucker, The Effective Executive (New York: HarperBusiness, 1967), p. 1 12.

Drucker's thoughts parallel the experience of the executives mentioned earlier who worked 20 fewer hours per week with a rise in productivity. The courage to reprioritize gave them more control over their lives. We might surmise that the quality of their personal lives rose in proportion to the additional time available to them.

At the other end of the spectrum, I have a client company where the average age of senior management is 38 years old. These guys are brilliant, with many holding MBAs from Stanford, Harvard and other prestigious schools. Working with this team during the past five years, I've sent notes to several of these managers who became first-time fathers. Talking with these men about life priorities is "real time" stuff.

One of the team members is 35, in his second marriage, and considered the creme-de-la-creme leader. He told me he had wanted to become a millionaire by the time he was 26, and he did; however, his first marriage failed because he gave himself over to his work and was never home. Now, with two children from his second marriage, he is still struggling with priorities. Fortunately he wants to change.

When I get together with the members of this management team we talk about life priorities. "Did you take that four-day vacation you said you would with your wife and kids? Did you do it without bringing your cell phone or laptop?"

It's a real struggle, but they begin to see the fruits of their efforts. They're around to see their new baby begin to crawl and then take first steps. They watch their kids in school plays and cheer them on at ball games. They're encouraged to use the corporate airplane so they can do turnarounds. They can leave Chicago in the morning and work in Des Moines until 5:00 with the intention of being home that evening.

The CEO of this company now insists that his direct reports take all their vacation time, including at least one uninterrupted two week vacation annually to ensure that the experience is physically and mentally refreshing. A hunger for more wholeness and completeness exists in the lives of a growing number of highly ambitious, talented leaders.

YOUR TURN AT THE PLOW:

If you are like most people, you want it all. You want money, position, respect, but you also want a loving family, close friends, and time for yourself. If you are honest with yourself I think you will find that what you really want is just to be happy.

What is your circumstance? Do you take good care of your health? Are you able to keep your work in perspective? Do you have friends other than business acquaintances that you see regularly? Is your family happy? Are you happy?

Don't panic. You can have it all. But first things first, if you are going to set up your field you have to keep your eyes on your future, your goal. Don't think about what you have done, do something new, right now.

Say it out loud:

"My first priority is to properly care for myself.

My second priority is my family.

My third priority is to be involved with people

that are important to me.

My fourth priority is my job.

Self.

Family.

Others.

Work."

Good. Now – let's plant some seeds.

PLANTING SEEDS

"A man reaps what he sows."

Galatians 6:7b NIV

On the hills behind my little farmhouse grow many varieties of wild fruit. To be specific, strawberries, ground cherries, gooseberries, a grape patch, one blueberry bush, and acres of black raspberries. I also occasionally benefit from three vegetables-gone-wild; asparagus, rhubarb and zucchini. And several other edible plants and nuts, such as walnuts, cattails and one everyone seems to have, dandelions (the young leaves make a spicy salad). All of these grow without me needing to plant or tend them. The zucchini was so virulent in fact that I needed to weed it out in order for other crops to grow. Undeterred it continued to grow wherever a seed landed, one year it was practically my most fruitful crop growing in every direction out of my compost heap.

If people grew like these plants we would have no need of good leadership. Fortunately people need help to grow. I say fortunately because it gives us a chance to have an influence regarding the character of those we have contact with. I have limited input into what grows in the woods and ponds. Most of the plants listed above produce smaller fruit than the grocery store variety, are rather scarce, sometimes diseased, and often grow in rather inconvenient places. Not only that, they are well known to the various critters that live in my woods, especially the white tail deer and black bear, so there's some stiff competition. Anyway, who wants to eat only zucchini and raspberries?

Every year I have the pleasure of *choosing* my produce. I choose my crops based on the time available to me to tend them, and wants of my friends and family. Demand is greatest for tomatoes. Every year I manage to grow a truckload of beautiful tomatoes and then I have the joy of handing out grocery bags full of them and assorted other crops. A good farmer realizes that he will reap what he sows... from his seed and his effort, a harvest to match.

When I am growing tomatoes from seed they start out in a way you may remember from grade school - an egg carton. Soil and one seed go into each cup, and then I cover the egg carton with plastic wrap held up by toothpicks. The amount of sunlight and the moisture level must be carefully monitored (I often lose seedlings during business trips). Once they are a few inches tall they get transplanted to the field. More watering and watching, but much less than when they were in egg cartons. Soon they are flowering, and the amount of maintenance they require is down to a couple hours twice a week... no big deal.

Growing people is the same, lots of investment up front, a chance for you to change their lives. Soon you find they take less of your time and are producing better results. Then one fine day you see them helping someone else grow, and the cycle goes on. The seed that was sown becomes a sower of seed, and the one who had sown the seed reaps a greater and greater harvest.

An effective leader embodies many characteristics and skills, but the heart of an effective leader is primarily that of a sower. Effective leaders sow themselves, their time, their enthusiasm, and their principles. Sowing, in fact all of farming, is an act of empowerment. You plow, plant, water and weed. To empower is to provide an atmosphere conducive to growth, giving of yourself in order to provide that plant every chance to succeed. All this in the hope of growing independent, effective, creative employees. Employees who are motivated to do their best because they are grateful, because they have a sense of pride in their company, and because they are happy.

THE NATURE OF EFFECTIVE LEADERSHIP

The first fundamental transformation of thinking required of American management is to develop new basic attitudes toward the intrinsic dignity and value of people, in particular, their "intrinsic motivation" to perform to their maximum capabilities. Management must empower its people in the deepest sense and remove the barriers and obstacles it has created that crush and defeat the inherent commitment, creativity and quality service that people are otherwise prepared to offer.[10]

The term "empowerment" is increasingly heard in modern leadership discussions. Astute leaders share their power in order to give their employees the latitude to fulfill their own potential. In the past, businesses designed hierarchies out of greed and fear. Managers were taught that a large part of their duty was to instill and maintain control over workers. Warren Bennis writes: "And you're not going to attract or retain a work force like that under those silly and obsolete forms of bureaucratic or command and control leadership. You cannot release the brainpower of any organization by using whips and chains. You get the best out of people

---

[10] Stephen R. Covey, Principle-Centered Leadership (New York: Summit Books, 1991), p. 264.

by empowering them, by supporting them, by getting out of their way."[11]

A NEW KIND OF LEADER

Leadership styles have not always lent themselves to the nurturing of the people in our companies. As recently as 1990, leaders were selected based on their résumés whether it was previous line management, financial, or sales and marketing experience. Today, leaders are much more often selected based on personal characteristics - their strategic thinking skills, their ability to relate to others, and their coaching and people skills. When discussing prospective team members, many of my clients say, "I'm not as concerned if she has the technical experience as I am that she's a good leader. She can learn the other stuff."

I call this the humanization of management – a huge change from our former experience based model of management. To further understand this shift, let's look

---

[11] Warren Bennis, On Becoming A Leader (New York: Addison-Wesley Publishing, 1989), p. xiii.

at the recent evolution of business leadership style in our country.

After World War II, the ensuing business boom created many management positions that were filled by veterans with a military mindset: top-down commands were received and passed along with the expectation of unquestioning obedience. Post-war workers, for the most part, were satisfied being part of America's great industrial machine. Our worldwide technological superiority expanded our economy at home and abroad. Lack of competition encouraged complacency of workers at all levels.

Decades later, with the shift in emphasis from heavy industrial to electronic and service-based businesses, the American advantage flattened. Our productivity slipped against that of foreign workers, revealing cracks in our system. Workers growing up through the social upheaval of the 1960s and 1970s were coming of age and weren't satisfied being unthinking workers obeying omnipotent bosses. A generation of largely college-educated workers wanted more input into the system.

The exercise of coercive power in rough economic times generally consisted of management "officers" threatening the "privates" with, "Produce, or else." This worked as a short-term tactic for boosting production but stifled long-term creativity.

The following table contains a few of the contrasting ideas between the old and new paradigms:

Old Model:	New Model:
Make me look good.	I'll help you do your best.
Produce, or else...	How can I help you improve?
You owe this company.	How can we benefit each other?
I'm a slave driver.	I'm an enabler.
Quarterly review.	Frequent progress checks.
Oppression.	Latitude.
Efficiency.	Effectiveness.

The old model of the boss-employee relationship was based on the employee making the boss look good.

Ultimately, that model doesn't work because there's nothing in it for the employee - other than possibly retaining his or her job.

A note about coercion: While coercion is rarely a necessity, it is an effective quality of leadership in some cases. One example is around issues of health and safety. If you're in a manufacturing setting, you may have protocols such as steel-toed shoes and helmets and protective clothing that you (and OSHA) mandate. This is not a debatable issue. It's in the interest of the organization and its employees to vehemently enforce these rules. Coercion, or top-down absolute control, should be seen only as an occasionally necessary tool rather than an operational style.

RELINQUISHING POWER

The single most major obstacle to implementing a leadership style of empowerment is trust. Empowering others requires that you trust them to do their jobs and this trust is extended up front when the employee is first hired, not withheld until "earned."

The kind of supervision commonly referred to as "micro-managing" is the antithesis of empowerment. Once you've provided yourself and other resources to help people be successful, you must step out of the way. This is often more difficult than it sounds. For example, you hire a person into a position (it might even be a position that you once had) and you find that initially that person is not as effective as you had hoped and you say to yourself, "Now I have to do their job too, because obviously I can do it better." The reality is, you can. But you need to allow the new person to do the job themselves, possibly poorly, in order for them to learn. This allows them the freedom to apply their own talents to the task, as well as your insights. The product is a hybrid, very likely improving the end result.

Additionally - and this is the beautiful part about this approach - you have nurtured the employee to become ultimately accountable for him or herself. Let's say that you're my boss, and you say to me, "John, I want to help you grow. Tell me, what do you need from me to help you?" So I tell you. And you provide it for me. But

I don't do the job. Then I am not performing because of myself alone. It's the ultimate form of accountability. Now, I'm responsible for my growth and results because my boss has been at my disposal, and has given me the resources I needed to succeed.

THE 2ND KEY TO SUCCESS: HELPING OTHERS SUCCEED

The whole concept of empowerment can be summed up with the words, "helping others succeed." Empowerment is not about corporate programs, mission statements or company mottos on coffee cups. It is about you, choosing to use some of your time and energy to help someone else be successful.

I don't mean to suggest that empowerment should not be built into company programs, mission statements or mottos – I think it should. But we should also not lose sight of the fact that the success or failure of a corporate initiative to empower its people comes down to one person trusting and helping another.

The first and second keys to success are inextricably tied. Employees who have their life priorities in order are able to concentrate on their work without being distracted by the debris in their lives. Employees who have been encouraged to live well by their company are not only free to concentrate, they want to. It doesn't matter what your company produces, if you encourage your employees to take care of themselves and go home on time to be with their family and friends, they will "believe" in the company. Imagine, if you haven't experienced it, what a single team of people who take pride in their company could accomplish.

There are four modes in which we can help others succeed: Modeling. Mentoring. Coaching moments. Building a corporate culture of empowerment.

MODELING

You can choose to be a mentor, but you can't choose to be a model. For good or ill, the very act of being present makes you one. Smart leaders understand this and recognize that everything they do and say (or don't say or do) will have an impact on those around them.

Any person in a leadership position is constantly being watched. Their behavior is always closely scrutinized. A wise leader will see that this is good, and make use of it.

Don't be surprised when your bad habits turn up in those around you. If you have been sowing crabgrass don't expect to harvest corn. Every day you are sowing yourself with every word and action. "Showing" is far more effective of a teaching tool than "telling." Display the behaviors you wish to see in your employees and colleagues. This is the foundation of all your efforts to help others succeed. Behave in a way contrary to what you expect in others and no one will take your leadership seriously.

One of the tools I make use of in my work is our Executive 360 Assessment. Its purpose is to help executives understand how they are viewed by those they work with, both in terms of their performance and social skills. It is amazing how unaware people are of the message they are sending.

The CEO of one of my client companies was concerned about one of the people who reported to him. The person in question had scheduled a few vacations but would report to the CEO a day or two before leaving and say, "Things are so busy. I just can't go." After the third cancelled vacation, the chairman even received a phone call from the executive's wife expressing her disappointment.

For the fourth time, the guy cancelled his vacation, claiming that he just had too much to do at the office.

Later that day, the CEO fired him.

Why? "I can't afford to have you as a model within this organization. Because you're a senior person, other people look up to you and may try to model behavior I think is inappropriate."

In the end, it doesn't matter whether or not this person expected similar behavior from the people around him. He was sending a clear message, family (and life) is less important than work. How do you think a person on his team might behave in order to impress this guy? Fortunately the CEO understood the power of modeling.

∾ Be aware of the message you are sending. If you have any doubt, use an assessment tool or (if you believe you will get an honest answer) start asking people.

∾ Ask yourself what behaviors are informing their opinions. If most everyone feels you are sending a particular message you can be assured that they are not just crazy – something you are doing is sending them the message.

∾ Don't just focus on the negative. Knowing what you are doing right is just as important, or more, than knowing what you are doing wrong. Often the way to overcome your weaknesses is by focusing on your strengths.

∾ Be yourself, or change yourself. Don't attempt to convey messages contrary to your character... it doesn't work.

Leaders are always on the lookout for "coaching moments" - using real moments to provide feedback "on the fly." Recognition and correction are best dealt with in the moment, on a daily basis. You would be surprised how little effect a quarterly review really has.

∽ Recognition: Coaching is a form of teaching, and that includes recognizing employee achievements. People, in general, don't consider money a principle motivator to do a job well. It may have some effect in the short term, but it is not sustainable. People need to be recognized verbally or in writing by their managers. Recognition, more than anything else, drives quality work.

Recently, a CEO client went backstage following an annual meeting and publicly congratulated the team who had helped him prepare for what was a successful meeting. He particularly singled out a woman who, for the first time, had taken the lead for the annual meeting preparation. His words were specific and generous. The recipients of his positive words were thrilled, and soon, countless employees in the organization heard about the CEO's expression of appreciation. One moment of recognition encouraged a company.

    ∽ Correction: If you want to motivate people to change their behavior because they did something wrong, give clear, specific, immediate feedback about observed behaviors. Handle this type of coaching moment discreetly, privately if possible. Make sure the feedback comes from a credible source. And remember to honor the person while rejecting the action. When you're giving feedback, never talk about attitude; always talk about behavior. People can't wrap their hands around attitude. Talking about behavior, on the other hand, reduces their defensiveness, which allows them to be more open to the message. Also, it gives them real information that they can use to reprioritize and choose a better course of action in the future.

    Lastly, if relevant, offer your assistance by way of guidance. Even if they turn the offer down, this sends them a clear message, "I value you personally and I'm willing to invest myself to see you succeed."

MENTORING

Mentoring represents a more formal process than modeling.

The whole concept of mentoring is often misconstrued. The image conjured up in most people's minds is that of the wizened master enlightening his headstrong protégé. Everything about this image is wrong.

➤ First, no one knows it all, wizened masters are rarely all they are cracked up to be. It reminds me of a line from the historical drama about the Cuban missile crisis, Thirteen Days. Faced with the daunting task of avoiding war with Russia, Kenny O'Donnell (played by Kevin Costner) says to John Kennedy, "There is no wise old man [...] there's just us."

You don't need to pretend you have reached enlightenment to mentor others. People generally don't expect others to have all the answers, more likely they are surprised to learn from someone else.

᠅ Second, mentoring works best when between people at a somewhat similar place in life, who have dealt with somewhat similar issues, in which one has more experience. This is why mentoring between managers and their direct reports is ideal – very often managers have occupied positions similar to those of their direct reports. Mentoring, however, can occur between a boss and subordinate, an employee and a leader from a different part of the organization, and sometimes between peers, assuming one has more experience.

᠅ Third, mentoring, if done with humility, is a two way street. Not only does mentoring reinforce the lessons we have learned, but if we are open to it, those we mentor can teach us a great deal as well.

᠅ Finally, a cautionary word, mentoring a single protégé is sometimes known around the water cooler by another name, favoritism. Choosing a single star (or just someone you like) to focus on can produce an environment of ill will. As a manager you are responsible for the results produced by *all* your direct reports. In order to take that responsibility seriously you must be seen as a potential mentor to them. The term "coach" better illustrates this point. You are a coach. You have a team. For any team to perform they have to have strong teamwork skills. To get the most out of your team you must coach them all, not play favorites, and build their cohesion *as a group.*

BUILDING A CORPORATE CULTURE OF EMPOWERMENT

My oldest son graduated from college with a degree in computer science that emphasized both hardware and software. When he got out of college, he had multiple job offers. He was in one position for three years, when a headhunter approached him with four offers from people who were interested in hiring him.

Here was a kid (he was only 24 at the time) being flattered and tempted with salaries far beyond those of his peers. But he said to me, "Dad, the offers are essentially the same. How should I choose?"

Later, he answered the question himself. He said, "Dad, I've decided to go back for another round of interviews with each company. But this time, I'm going to search for the right environment for me." Essentially, he interviewed them. And he finally chose an organization that was absolutely committed to his growth and development. It's an organization that allowed him the potential of one day off per month (that's one out of every 20 working days) just to learn more about computers. They even occasionally gave him a plane ticket so he could travel for learning.

This is an example of what's happening more and more in American business. More people are putting their names out there, even though they're currently employed, because they're searching for the right environment for themselves.

Effective leaders and organizations give attention to the environment they create. The challenge lies in nurturing an environment that makes employees want to excel. Effective leaders realize that, in effect, they must persuade their employees to buy into the company, in order for their employees to take ownership of their work. One of the most crucial ways a company can sell itself to its people is through empowerment. Prove to them that not only *can* they contribute in a meaningful way, you *want* them to, and watch their energy level and contributions rise.

Last year, one of my new client companies released a report about their poor employee retention rate. According to this report, the dollar cost of losing productive workers was more than $75 million <u>over</u> industry average. The number one reason given by workers during their exit interviews? Lack of empowerment.

Succeed in producing a culture of empowerment and talent will wait in line for a chance to be a part of it. And when an organization is filled with employees who truly want to be there, magic happens.

One of my client companies asked me to attend a two-day orientation program for new employees. The gentleman who led the session had been with the company for more than 35 years. He was a gray-haired, grandfatherly type who said, "During the next two days, I'm going to tell you everything you need to know about this company."

In an orderly fashion, he laid out all the information intended to bring these people up-to-speed about the organization. He talked about the history, the good times and the bad, and he eventually outlined goals, expectations, values, and objectives - all the information they could ever want or need.

I was having lunch with the CEO some time later, and in the course of our discussion he said, "You know quite a bit about the company."

I replied, "True. I've had a number of experiences with your company, including one that was a little bit troubling. I attended portions of a two-day orientation where the leader talked for more than four hours about the history of the company and about all the expectations it has for the new employees. He threw a ton of information at us - too much, in fact, for any new employee to retain and I'm not sure how much of the information was really important to the new hires."

As a result of this conversation, and others I was part of, the company decided to revamp its orientation sessions. The new policy states that orientations for new employees must be conducted by those who have been on the job for no more than 18 months. In other words, new employees are now orientating new employees.

Months later, I attended the new format orientation session - which was only a half-day instead of two. The young woman leading the orientation stood up nervously and said, "I've been employed by this company about 15 months, and the reason I'm here is to help you be successful in your work. As time goes along, when you need to know more, we'll get together as a group and we'll learn those things, too. But first, does everyone know where the bathrooms are?"

The atmosphere of the meeting was entirely different - more relaxed and congenial. Not only were the new employees working productively after only a half-day of orientation, but also from day one they knew that their orientation leader was there to help them succeed.

As word got around, bosses at all levels of the organization began finding ways of incorporating additional forms of empowerment into the corporate structure.

Today, they have a waiting list of people hoping to be hired.

It's Time To Start Planting

Farming is all about growing plants. To have a successful farm, you have to enjoy getting dirty. Leadership is all about growing people. Leadership involves seriously interacting with people in order to help them succeed. Many leaders try to keep themselves above the fray and miss their best chance to be effective. Your employees need your attention and guidance in order to have the skills and desire to excel.

Don't be deceived, you have something to offer. The most important seed you can sow is your behavior reflective of your life priorities. The very act of putting yourself out there is encouraging to others. Let them know you want to help them succeed and they will eventually tell you how you can help them. Take the risk, put a welcome mat out, and roll up your sleeves – it's time to get real. If you don't, who will? After all, there is no wise old man... there's just us.

Pick up your seed sack and say:
"I will trust in the intrinsic nature of people to perform to their maximum potential.
I will assist in unlocking this potential by choosing empowerment over coercion.
I will generously share my power, my time and myself, in order to improve the lives of others.
I will help others succeed by living my life as I know I should, knowing that the world is watching."

PULLING WEEDS

"I went past the field of the sluggard,

past the vineyard of the man who lacks judgment;

thorns had come up everywhere,

the ground was covered with weeds,

and the stone wall was in ruins."

Proverbs 24:30-31 NIV

"Balance," for most executives the word is almost spiritual, something akin to "nirvana" and just as elusive. How is it possible to give your all at work and still find time for family, friends and yourself?

Balance, a wealth of books have told us, can be achieved through greater efficiency, goal setting, or achieving a state of mind. These approaches may work for some people whose lives are not terribly out of balance. Most of us, however, need more drastic measures.

In a perfect world, a plant would need only sun, water and soft earth. But the earth, like our lives, is filled with weeds.

In my defense, it was a really hot day. I had taken to the task of weeding a flower garden around my front porch. Taking a break, I stood back to admire my work, not a weed in sight. Then the thought struck me, weren't there supposed to be flowers in this flower garden?

Weeding is all about careful observation. Telling the difference between a weed and a morning glory is easy enough once the morning glory is grown (at which stage weeding isn't as crucial). However, the task can be tricky when your plants are young - and vulnerable. Knowing every form of weed is practically impossible, that is why a farmer must be thoroughly familiar with his crops. If he can identify the young plants he is trying to save then weeding is a cinch – just rip out everything else.

So what are we trying to save?

Our crop is time well spent. Time invested in our physical and emotional well-being. Time invested in our families and our friends. And time invested in furthering our careers by helping others and applying the best of us to our organizations.

So what is a weed?

A weed is anything that distracts us from investing our time well. Anything that causes an imbalance between how we spend our time and our life priorities. Anything that is a waste of our time.

YOUR MONEY OR YOUR LIFE:

We've all heard the saying, "Time is money." This is true in terms of business strategy. Outside of business strategy a better saying is, "Time is life." If something is a waste of your time, it is a waste of your *life*. Time well spent is *life* well spent.

Thinking of time in terms of life reminds us that our time is precious and should not be wasted. If you can gain control of your time, you have gained control of your life. This is our objective in this chapter – nothing less than learning to gain control of life in order to live the life you want.

"Money can be spent and reearned; we can lose all of our savings or our job and then come back again and take another shot at it. Time, however, is the most precious currency of life, and how we spend it reflects what we truly value. Once we have spent it, it is gone forever!"[12]

Time is our most precious commodity. Money is a mere pittance compared to time. How much would you pay for another year of life? Maybe not too much right now, but just wait, very likely a time will come when you would give every last cent for another month, another week, one more day in the light.

THE 3RD KEY TO SUCCESS: HAVING A SENSE OF URGENCY

It was a minor miscalculation. I had hooked up a large mower deck to the back of my tractor and was

---

[12] Richard J. Leider, The Power of Purpose: Creating meaning in your life and work, 1997 (Berrett-Koehler, San Francisco).

mowing some of the tougher grass surrounding one of my gardens. This particular garden had been expanded that year, a factor that I failed to take into account. I mowed just as I always had, following a familiar pattern, and consequently I was off target by about a foot. The result was impressive – an entire row of fully grown Swiss chard lettuce chopped down to the stumps, leaving a fifteen foot long salad, that no doubt the rabbits enjoyed.

In work and life we seek the route of least resistance, those familiar patterns and routines that over time have become like comfortable friends to us. Unfortunately the route of least resistance almost always leads to regret. We get through life expending just enough energy to get by, but not enough energy to excel. We do what is expected of us, instead of what we have to offer. We do what is simple instead of what is complex. We do what gratifies us most in the instant, instead of what would make us happy in the long run. And in the end we look at the life we mowed down to the stumps and wonder what went wrong.

Life is short. We have one chance, one shot, at achieving the life we want. We may have only a little influence over the length of our life but we are fully in control of its quality. In order to succeed at business and life you must remove behaviors and activities which are holding you back and maximize those which will help you soar – always keeping in mind that the clock is ticking.

The concept of weeding is essential in order to succeed at work and life. Our desires and other demands for our time will always exceed the amount of time we have available to us. You can achieve the life you want, but only through sacrifice, this is the element missing from most approaches to time management. If you try to do everything, you will wind up with nothing.

Think ahead to your latter years, imagine you've retired. Where do you want to be? *Who* do you want to be? Who do you want to be with you? Even if all you want is, like me, a loving family, a quiet cabin on a lake, and the knowledge that you have helped people succeed, you will still need to make sacrifices to achieve it.

The goal is nothing less than your life's happiness, the challenge... balance.

DEFINING BALANCE:

Do you remember that doughnuts commercial from a few years back? A pudgy, sleepy eyed, doughnuts baker would walk in the door of the bakery and say, "Time to make the doughnuts." Every night as he left he would say, "I made the doughnuts." This happened over and over with less and less sleep in between. Eventually he woke up to "make the doughnuts" so early that he ran into himself leaving after having "made the doughnuts."

Time and again I meet exasperated executives who have more work to do than there are hours in a day. And like the poor baker they are exhausted, suffering, and no fun to be around. What these executives need is balance.

But before we can proceed in taking steps to gain it, we must define what it is.

Balance, in essence, is a matter of properly allocating our time between time spent working and time spent living, so that the amount of time spent working enhances, not overwhelms, the rest of our life.

For some people this distinction has been blurred, "But I love my job. For me, working *is* living." I have found that the real reason many people "love" their job is because it enables them to avoid serious issues in their life outside of work. But let's say, for the sake of argument, that you are a person who actually *does* love your job. You can hardly believe they pay you for something you would do for free because it's so fun. I have some bad news for you; employment is very rarely a permanent part of life. Very likely, you will retire.

Right now you are creating, brick by brick, the house you will soon be living in. The more disproportionately you invest your time in your job, the less you will be left with when it is gone. No matter how much you may like your job – living, building a life, occurs primarily at home.

Another more serious false conception is that living can be put off till later. People say to me, "I'll have time to live when I retire." They talk about trips they will take with their spouses, spending time with children and grandchildren, getting together with friends, writing novels, having parties, etc.

This brings to mind one of my favorite sayings, "Life is what happens to you while you're making plans for the future."

In my experience, executives who live for their work, and hold out on truly living till retirement, experience unhappy and short retirements. Some common factors for this are:

A starved marriage turns into a cold one when the couple suddenly finds themselves together almost all day, every day. The skills and motivation necessary to enjoy their relationship have been lost due to neglect.

Children are often absent, resenting the years of neglect they experienced. Also, modeling their parents' behavior, they feel they don't have the time to visit.

Old friends have, meanwhile, found more reliable friends. Friends from work turn out to be not nearly as close, or compatible, as you had thought, once the commonality of work is removed.

Life is difficult to enjoy due to health problems from years of ignoring health concerns and physical fitness.

Vacations are far less enjoyable than expected because of marital tension, poor health, and lack of interested people with whom to share the experience.

Without the structure of the work environment their grandiose plans to write that book are quickly abandoned.

Without work to provide a purpose for their existence, and without the strong support of love ones to provide new purpose, the person feels aimless, sometimes even worthless (this last factor is especially prevalent among males who were in senior management positions).

The final result: Facing some, or all, of these issues the person becomes depressed and reclusive. Serious health problems soon follow and all too often an early death.

Living cannot be put off till later, nor can a life be built at work. This means we need to balance our time spent working with our time spent living if we are to avoid regret.

So what does balance look like? Let's examine how time is spent in the day of an average working adult:

Seven to eight hours are spent sleeping. One hour is spent bathing and dressing. Two hours are spent eating. Plus one to two hours to run errands and do chores. So it takes eleven to thirteen hours a day just to keep our motors running.

On workdays one hour is spent getting to and from work and eight hours a day are spent at work. So in the average workday, twenty to twenty two hours are taken up fulfilling basic priorities, leaving two to four hours free time.

In an average week, assuming a five day work week, this means approximately 45 hours are spent working or commuting, leaving 39 hours free – not too bad.

Take, however, the case of the company I mentioned in the first chapter, the one in which the executives were averaging a 72 hour work week. Total time spent working or commuting, assuming a six day work week: 78 hours. Total free time: six hours.

Six hours. Can you raise children in six hours a week? How about nurture a loving marriage? I'm willing to bet those six hours were spent either fending off arguments from their spouse, or sacked in front of the television, exhausted.

When our lives are in balance, work is an essential crop, enriching our lives. When our lives are out of balance, work is a virulent and destructive weed.

Excessive work chokes our time, eliminating many quality life experiences and cutting years from our lives.

Without so much as a whimper we let our lives be choked by our jobs.

CHOOSING BALANCE:

I expect at this point some of you may be thinking, "I can't cut my hours – I'm expected to work as much as I am." In most cases it isn't an issue of "can't" but "too scared to try." People are afraid that they will be thought of as a slacker, criticized more harshly and miss promotion opportunities. In many corporate cultures this is true.

You have three options:

• Make a stand on your hours and deal with whatever may come. If you are a more assertive person than most this may appeal to you, but it's risky. Fortunately for the rest of us, there are better options.

• Get a new job with a company that has a more empowering corporate culture, or take a new job with a clear understanding of the hours expected of you. This option has the greatest assurance of getting you to where you want to be, and for some people it will be their only option, but there is a less extreme course of action.

    ~ Influence the corporate culture. If there is a central message to this book it is this:

> "People who re-order their *life priorities* are able to concentrate on *work* without being distracted by the debris in their lives. By making their work a lower priority the quality and consistency of their work improves."

The first step in influencing the corporate culture: Spread the word. Make sure everyone hears what you're thinking, your boss, colleagues, and direct reports. Call it a "productivity experiment," hand out this book, whatever it takes to get the word out.

Step two: Talk about your family and ask about other's families. There is nothing like being reminded that you have a family to bring things into perspective. For most people higher productivity simply means longer hours. Prepare yourself for some strange reactions as you bring family and productivity together in one conversion. To a lot of people it will sound too good to be true – turning lead into gold.

Step three: Encourage your direct reports to work reasonable hours. If you cut your hours without encouraging your direct reports to do the same, you are a fraud and may have a mutiny on your hands.

Step four: Go home. As with most new habits, the first week will be the most difficult. You may feel guilty or overwhelmed by thoughts of all the work you are leaving unfinished. Deadlines will loom larger than before, casting an even more imposing shadow. As with everything worth doing in life, it will take courage.

Step five: Prove yourself. This is really the key, isn't it? If working less and living more doesn't improve your work, or the work of your direct reports, things will eventually return to the way they were – long hours, no life.

Having more time to live makes a difference in the quality of one's life and in the quality of one's work, but how big of a difference depends on what you do with that time, which is where we turn now.

HAVING A SENSE OF URGENCY IN YOUR PRIVATE LIFE

In the first key to success I outline four priorities, the first three are in the realm of the private life:

1st Priority: Self-sustenance. Which includes taking care of your health, relaxing, having fun, and being with others.

2nd Priority: Family. Taking time to be with your family, and connecting with them on a real level.

3rd Priority: People who are important to me. Participating in groups that are meaningful to you, and taking the time to nurture friendships.

In this part of our conversation we'll be talking about the first two priorities, self-sustenance and family, this is because the first two priorities need to be touched on almost daily, the third does not.

Most people seem to accept the need for self-sustenance to be a daily activity, even if they really only intend to follow through with the health aspect of it. The second priority, family, causes more of a stir. With only four hours at the most to spare on weekdays (two to three hours more likely), why not just connect on the weekends? Two reasons: First, the relationships you have with the members of your family are like no other relationships in life, they define who you are as a person, for better or worse. To succeed as a spouse or father, or mother, is a greater success than anything you accomplish in the rest of life. And unlike success in most other arenas of life, that accomplishment will reward you more and more as time passes. These relationships are too important for anything less than daily involvement with those who are waiting for you at home. In business terms this is the ultimate ROI (Return On Investment).

Second, your family needs you. The moments that deepen our family relationships do not neatly schedule themselves on the weekends. The bruises and joys of life happen without fair warning. Whether they are willing to admit it or not, until your children leave home, they want you to notice them, comfort them and love them every day. If this is even true of teenagers imagine how much more true it is of your spouse. A weekend parent or spouse runs the risk of hearing the dreaded words, "You were never there for me."

OUR CROP – TIME WELL SPENT:

To some it may seem as if I am suggesting the impossible, "Exercise, relax, play, socialize, and be there for my family... in three hours a day?"

Yes, even in two. The trick is seeking out those activities that provide the greatest return in the least amount of time – these activities are your crops.

Even though self-sustenance is your first priority, most likely it is the family priority you will find most challenging to fulfill. You may be able to think of pages of high quality activities *you* would want to do, but unless they interest your family as well, you are still leaving them out in the cold. A good way to avoid this result is to focus on one family member at a time. What do they like to do? What have they shown an interest in? What do we have in common? What do I know about their life right now? And, of course, it never hurts to ask.

An activity can be high quality without being fun or relaxing for either of you. For instance, doing housework together, grocery shopping, or helping one of your children with their homework. These types of activity are only beneficial when either you are helping them, or they have offered of their own freewill to help you. Commandeering someone to help you clean the garage may get the job done quicker, but it's unlikely you have improved your relationship in the process. Instead try making garage cleaning a regular chore for your children and then offering to help with it. Sneaky, but satisfying.

On weekdays the emphasis is on quick activities that require little or no prep time. Going to the zoo is probably an activity best saved for the weekend.

Here are a few high quality activities to start you thinking:

- ⤜ Running with your spouse every morning.
- ⤜ Sitting and listening as one of your children practices an instrument.
- ⤜ Playing a game (board game, video game, pool, whatever).
- ⤜ Going shopping (don't forget, if you wind up carrying bags around the mall it's exercise).
- ⤜ Going with your family to a sporting event one of your children is involved in.
- ⤜ Practicing a sport with one of your children.
- ⤜ Working on a project or hobby with your spouse.
- ⤜ Working for a few hours on that tree fort you and your child are building.
- ⤜ Driving around the neighborhood looking at Christmas tree light displays.
- ⤜ Having a snowball fight.

As you can see, it would be easy to provide for your self-sustenance and connect with your family with just two of these.

Of course not every day will give you an opportunity to do high quality activities, but every day gives you opportunities to have high quality *moments*. Even if you only have twenty minutes to spare in a day, you can still sneak these in:

- Dump a load of warm laundry on someone.
- Tell a joke.
- Challenge someone to a pushup contest.
- Make up a completely ludicrous story about what happened at work today (hint at an alien conspiracy) and try to tell it with a straight face.
- Tell someone how you really feel about something important in your life.
- Bring home a bouquet of flowers... and pizza.
- Spontaneously serve everyone ice cream.

~ Every few days tell everyone you've discovered the meaning to life... and make it completely different every time.

~ Tell someone that you love them, and say it in a way that lets them know you really mean it.

PULLING CRABGRASS:

Crabgrass is amazing stuff, if it wasn't such a pain I would probably think rather highly of it. Crabgrass spreads primarily by root growth, wherever a crabgrass root touches the surface a new plant shoots up. This means thousands of crabgrass plants can in fact be all one interconnected plant, with a root system that looks like a diagram of the internet. This brings us to why it is such a pain, pulling up mature crabgrass is like trying to pull a chain link fence through six inches of soil.

To this point most of the weeding I have suggested has been relatively painless. Hopefully you have identified your crops and intend to keep them within their proper boundaries to prevent them from becoming weeds. The next step is simple, rip out everything else. Unfortunately the leap between knowing what you need to remove from your life, and actually removing it, can be a large one. It is time to put on your gloves and get dirty – we're pulling crabgrass.

    ∾ Driving alone in your automobile.

Your commute, that space of time we spend between work and home can become so much a part of our existence that we fail to recognize its impact on our lives.

I consider a half hour commute to be normal. It is difficult, especially in large cities, to live much closer to work than that. An hour, however, is rarely necessary. If it takes you an hour or more to get to work, you should seriously consider either moving or getting a new job.

No, I'm not kidding.

That extra five hours represents one seventh of your total free time if you work a forty hour work week. Not only that, the monotony and frustration drains your energy both coming and going, making it difficult to be actively present at either home or work. Most of all, it more than doubles your chance of being in a car accident and possibly losing all the time you have left.

Of course a highly legitimate option is to leave the driving to a professional. Take a bus, train, or hire a driver. This allows you to regain what would otherwise be lost time. On the way to work get a start on that project. If this works well, leave work early. On the way home get everything set for tomorrow so you can leave your concerns from work behind.

  ⁊   Wireless incarceration.

I once saw a cartoon in which a man on a tropical beach says to his wife, "Ah, this is the life. Just you, me, my pager, my cell phone, my portable fax...."

The humor in this cartoon is not lost on many busy people. More and more we live in an instant access world. Thanks to the wireless communication revolution we can now be interrupted by a telemarketer while white water rafting.

In order to be fully present and engaged in life while away from work I strongly suggest screening your calls. I started screening my calls out of necessity. A few years ago I finally decided I couldn't put off buying a fax machine for my home any longer. I spent too much time away from the office to do without one. Since I live back in the woods at the end of seriously out dated phone line, call waiting is not an option and the connection is tenuous at best. In order to ensure I can receive a fax I have to let the fax/answering machine get the call.

At first I found this to be a nuisance and tried to get the phone company to fix the problem, but since it would involve replacing a mile of underground cable just for me, it didn't happen. Looking back, I'm glad. Once I was over my habit of always answering the phone I realized that most the calls I received, I wouldn't have wanted to pick up. I also found that, by not picking up, I now had time to prepare myself for the calls I choose to return. So not only was I not being constantly interrupted by the phone, I also improved the quality of the work I delivered by phone.

Some suggestions:

Turn off the pager and cell phone when you leave work.

Turn off the ringer on all but one phone at home. There's nothing like having phones all over the house ringing in unison to make you run for the phone, if simply to shut it up.

Discontinue your voice mail and buy an answering machine. Even with caller ID the only way to be certain of the identity of the caller is to hear their voice, and the tone of their voice is sometimes crucial in deciding if you want to pick up.

Set your answering machine to pick up on two rings instead of four. This will cut down on the urge to pick up the phone in order to shut it up, and it makes it virtually impossible to get to the phone before the answering machine gets it, so why try?

ॐ Public broadcasting syndrome.

According to a recent study, the average adult American watches 4.37 hours of television a day.[13] That adds up to about 30 ½ hours a week. As I suggested earlier, the average working adult has around 39 hours of free time a week in which to build a life. Even if you add in two hours for watching television during meals, the average working adult still wastes more than half of their free time watching television.

Jean-Louis Servan-Schreiber in his classic book "The Art of Time" observed,

"Now, the past four decades have not seen a shortening of the work week. So on top of our forty work hours, television's 10 percent of the week's hours are taken from the hours remaining – either *instead of* activities like sleep, recreation, reading, and puttering, or *along with* meals, family time, work around the house, but always *at the*

---

[13] 2002 *MARS OTC/DTC Pharmaceutical Study.*

expense of things like conversation, affectivity, concentration, and inner calm."[14]

If this is the case, then why do we do it? The short answer is, to escape. To escape from our stress, to escape from family responsibilities, to escape from our own self-critical minds. Karl Marx said that religion was the opiate of the masses. I disagree, television is.

"The term "TV addiction" is imprecise and laden with value judgments, but it captures the essence of a very real phenomenon. Psychologists and psychiatrists formally define substance dependence as a disorder characterized by criteria that include spending a great deal of time using the substance; using it more often than one intends; thinking about reducing use or making repeated unsuccessful efforts to reduce use; giving up important social,

[14] Jean-Louis Servan-Schreiber, The Art of Time, (Addison-Wesley Publishing Company) 1988, p. 16.

family or occupational activities to use it; and reporting withdrawal symptoms when one stops using it." [15]

Further:

"As one might expect, people [watching television feel] relaxed and passive." "What is more surprising is that the sense of relaxation ends when the set is turned off, but the feelings of passivity and lowered alertness continue. Survey participants commonly reflect that television has somehow absorbed or sucked out their energy, leaving them depleted. They say they have more difficulty concentrating after viewing than before. In contrast, they rarely indicate such difficulty after reading. After playing sports or engaging in hobbies, people report improvements in mood. After

[15] Robert Kubey and Mihaly Csikszentmihalyi, "Television Addiction Is No Mere Metaphor," Scientific American, February 23, 2002.

watching TV, people's moods are about the same or worse than before." "Thus, the irony of TV: people watch a great deal longer than they plan to, even though prolonged viewing is less rewarding."[16]

Watching television is more likely than any other single activity to derail your plans to build a life. Here are some suggestions to keep this weed under control:

Don't turn on the television the moment you walk in the door. This is such an ingrained habit for some people that it will be hard to break. Find some other higher quality activity to get involved in to complete the work-to-home transition.

Choose one or two nights a week that your family feels the best shows are on to watch television. The other days of the week are not "TV days."

Pay attention to the effect particular shows are having on you and your family. Which shows cause you to be less social, which ones more?

---

[16] Robert Kubey and Mihaly Csikszentmihalyi, "Television Addiction Is No Mere Metaphor," Scientific American, February 23, 2002.

Don't look at TV show listings. What you don't know is on, you won't miss.

Watch movies together instead, and play it up. Watching a movie with your whole family can be a very social event if everyone gets involved. Make snacks, wrap up in quilts, and give yourself enough time to talk when it is over.

≈ Buying time.

Doing chores can be a rewarding experience, it can be relaxing, a time to connect with others, and bring us a sense of satisfaction. However, chores are usually just a pain in neck. Is changing the oil in your car a rewarding experience? No? Go to a quick lube garage. How about mowing your lawn? There is probably a neighborhood kid who could use the money.

A lot of people feel guilty using their money in this way, as if it means they are lazy or inept. I mean, shouldn't all men do their own home repair, and all women their own house cleaning? Not if they have the means to avoid it. Think about it this way, nearly the worst way you can spend your money is on things that will consume your time, and nearly the best way is on things that will grant you time. This is actually one of the best ways in which money can be used.

When the choice comes down to your money or your life, whenever you can, choose your life.

TIME TO FLY:

Take a moment to imagine it: You've made a stand on your hours. Your relationship with your family is improving. Then one day it hits you, you're happy.

You don't need more money to be happy, you don't need another promotion to be happy, or your face on the cover of Fortune. In fact, you don't need much of anything from your job besides just enough money to get by. So what's the incentive?

In a nutshell, the incentive is the realization of your legacy. When all is said and done, what you take away from your time in the marketplace will be what you left behind – the lives you affected, the impact that had on the company, and the change that made in the world.

Only one person can make your unique contribution – you. So get to it! Don't let yourself go to your grave with your music still inside of you.

HAVING A SENSE OF URGENCY IN YOUR PROFESSIONAL LIFE:

Think for a moment, what are you best at, what are your skills, your strengths? What seems to come more easily for you than others?

Now, reflect on what you do in your present position, does it make use of your talents?

The rate of change in the marketplace is steadily increasing. It used to be that you could sell a product, year after year, with only minor improvements slowly introduced. Now seemingly every product is in strict competition for sales. It's not just computers that suffer from rapid obsolescence. Companies that make everything from toothbrushes to golf clubs must innovate or perish. Even such time-honored and stable industries as electricity, car insurance, and newspapers have been shaken up. The days of the untouchable "fat cats" are over. More and more consumers are ignoring the label. They want better products, cheaper products, and most of all, new products. And, it turns out, they actually *think* before they buy.

On the corporate level having a sense of urgency means being one step ahead of your competition. Few companies can stay on top for long without reinventing themselves every few years. Your success is tied to your company's success, and your company's success requires excellence in every department, at every level. This is why it is essential to be doing what you do best.

Sometimes a fair amount of the responsibilities of any position will not be within one person's areas of strength. The goal is to free yourself from these responsibilities as much as possible in order to take on responsibilities at which you will be able to excel.

The most immediate way of doing this is through delegation. By seeking out people with the right talents you're doing yourself a favor and you're doing them a favor. You're also making it possible for the work to get done better than you could have done it, thus helping the company.

Delegation, however, is not always an option, and for these occasions you need to learn five skills: Saying no. Saying yes. Reaching for the biggest weed first. Interrupting interruptions. Celebrating Independence Day.

LEARN TO SAY NO:

No doubt you have heard this suggestion many times, there's a reason, it's crucial. The only other options are saying yes to everything, or saying that you'll get back to them... and hoping they forget they asked.

Let's role play: If you say yes to everything more and more people will come to you with their requests. You will say yes to more people. Your workload will exceed all reasonable ability to accomplish the work, but not before you run yourself ragged trying to do the impossible. Again, the final result: You will let people down and endanger your career.

Saying yes indiscriminately is instant gratification, with long-term repercussions. Saying yes indiscriminately is akin to choosing not to weed. On the one hand, you don't have to get up from your chair. On the other hand, your crops begin fighting a losing battle. Momentary pleasure, long-term pain.

When you say yes, in the moment you get praise and affirmation, "Thank you so much, you have no idea what this means to me." You get a chance to pity yourself, "*Now* how am I going to do it all!" You have the promise of pity and praise from others, "Wow, with all you have to do, I can't believe you took on the Anderson account too! I bet you are the hardest working person in the company." You get to think good things about yourself, "Chuck is so over worked, it was right of me to sacrifice myself for him and his family." You get to imagine the praise you will receive for doing the job better, "I can't believe what you did with the Anderson account! Chuck does alright but you are a master!" You get to procrastinate on a project you are frustrated or bored with, "I can come back fresh to the Jamison account when I'm done with this." You get to avoid problems at home, "Sorry Honey, I'll be late at work again. I have the Anderson account, no one else can do it. I'm sure to get a promotion out of it though."

And, most of all, you get to avoid negative feedback and guilt from the person who is making the request, "But I have a new baby I have barely seen and everyone else has said no!" "My job is on the line here." "I work 70 hours a week, and you leave every day at five."

So to avoid momentary discomfort you say yes, and when you can't do it all, you let others down. You break your promises. Your quality of work goes down. You undermine your ability to contribute meaningfully. You are thought of poorly. You miss promotion. You may even get fired.

Few people have the fortitude to simply say no without an explanation. This is probably not a really good idea anyway. In most cases either an explanation or some assurance that you have considered the proposal is in order. The trick is being prepared to do or say one of three things:

    ❧ The direct approach. Explain what your screening criteria is and why this project is out of your area of talent. This is most likely the best approach as you are setting an example of good decision making.

    ❧ Excuse yourself. If the direct approach is a little too direct for you this is probably your next best choice; memorize or keep handy a list of the projects you are working on and your job responsibilities.

    ❧ Forestall. Memorize this phrase, "I'll look into it and get back to you tomorrow." If you don't trust yourself to be able to make the right choice in the moment or feel you might just cave in under pressure this gives you the chance to think it through and bolster your courage if you intend to say no. But *do* get back to them tomorrow.

Learn to Say Yes:

Sometimes saying no to a task is not an option, regardless of how unsuited it is for you, like when it comes from your boss. There are several ways of saying yes conditionally that may be advantageous in these situations:

If you think you might be able to find someone more suited for the task than yourself you might try offering to do so.

Maybe there is a part of the project you could agree to that is more aimed at your talents. A warning though, make sure you are aware of the amount of collaboration necessary, and with whom it would be.

If the request is coming from your boss, ask how to prioritize this new project with your other projects, and make sure you mention what those other projects are. If the new project ranks pretty low he may give it to someone else, or it may provide you with the opportunity to suggest someone else.

REACH FOR THE BIGGEST WEED FIRST:

Most people do projects that are familiar and simple first, and put off what is unfamiliar or complicated. Unfortunately, in a constantly changing marketplace, the most important projects are likely to be unfamiliar and complicated, and therefore get delayed.

When you show up for work you should have one thing in your mind, making gains on your most important project. People waste the best part of the day "warming up." They get some coffee, return a few phone calls, finish a few minor tasks, etc. Then, when they are ready, they work on the big, important task for fifteen minutes and break for lunch. And on it goes....

Try this: Make a list of your projects from most to least important. Then on another sheet of paper write down the steps involved in completing your most important project. On a third sheet of paper write down the step you intend to work on tomorrow, and put the other two lists away. Leave the paper with tomorrow's step written on it, smack-dab on the middle of your desk. When you get to work, hang up your coat, sit down and read your step for the day. Then, quick, before you get distracted, pull out the project materials and do it.

This is often much harder than it sounds, so be prepared for an inner struggle. This kind of radical anti-procrastination flies in the face of all our years of rationalizing our way out of direct action. Believe it or not, procrastination is so ingrained in us that forcing yourself to be working on your most critical task within sixty seconds of walking in the door can produce quite a rush. This is a very helpful jump-start if you're not a morning person.

INTERRUPTING INTERUPTIONS:

A manager gets interrupted every seven to eight minutes,[17] how is it possible to get anywhere with so little consecutive time? Projects that require a great deal of thought (most really important projects do) are at a

---

[17] Jean-Louis Servan-Schreiber, The Art of Time, (Addison-Wesley Publishing Company) 1988, p. 26.

special disadvantage since it can take ten to fifteen minutes of concentrated thought to "get into it" again. The solution is to sanctify some time during your day as "project time." "Project time" is time set aside to work on your most important project, free from interruptions. This works best before lunch, as the chance for important interruptions increases as the day progresses. Interruptions come in two main varieties, phone calls, and "walk-ins."

Dealing with phone calls is easy, set your answering machine (or voice mail) to pick up in two rings and don't check your messages until after your project time is over. Same for email, don't check it until after your project time is over.

"Walk-ins" are tougher weeds. There are two good methods of dealing with "walk-ins," have open and closed office hours, or keep an appointment calendar. Open and closed office hours are simpler, especially if you lack a full time assistant to take appointments for you. The trick to making open and closed office hours work is to make sure that everyone knows when they are.

Putting a sign on your door may look tacky but is guaranteed effective, especially if you actually close your door.

Taking appointments for later in the day, or the following day, is more complicated and pretty much requires a full time assistant. It has, however, two significant advantages: First, the would-be-interrupter now has time to think about the nature of their visit, increasing the possibility that they will be able to get to the point quickly and know what they are talking about. Second, given some time to think about the problem they might figure it out for themselves, encouraging their independence.

Lastly, if you want people to respect your time, you need to respect theirs. Ask others if it is a good time before jumping into a conversation with them, encourage others to set aside project time, and whenever the occasion arises, defend others time from interruptions. Respect other people's time and you won't need to fight for time of your own.

No matter how much you try you will not be able to stem interruptions unless you empower your direct reports to work independently. Having people ask you for your opinion constantly may make you feel important, but it will also get in the way of your success and theirs. Micromanaging, with its fine-toothed criticism, trains people to be dependant. In order to avoid criticism the employee needs to check in often, which is what a micromanager wants – a sense of control.

Encouraging independence requires the exact opposite, macromanaging. The first step in macromanaging is hiring for talent. Education and experience are important factors but they pale in comparison to talent – anyone can be trained if they have the right talent. An unskilled but talented person may require more attention up front, but in the long run they produce better results with less supervision.

Macromanaging also involves a big picture view of goal setting. Make sure your direct reports know what their highest priority assignment is. Make sure they know the deadline. Offer your assistance up front, but leave the details for them to figure out. When they come to you for help, ask questions to help them come to their own conclusions. Balance criticism of their work with praise regarding their character. Criticism dealt with too heavy a hand can lead to insecurity and dependence, if instead you take a high view of others, they will try to live up to your expectations.

SEIZE THE DAY:

Let's say you've done it – you're in a position that maximizes your talents. You've learned to say no and you've managed to quell interruptions. You just finished your last major project and (stop the presses!) you have some free time. What do you do?

I'll start with what not to do. Don't revert to micromanaging mode and go around checking up on everyone. Don't fall into the trap of doing busy work during your project time. And don't give up your project time until another major project comes around.

Instead use your project time to find ways of applying your talents in a search for excellence. Here are some ways of bringing your talents to bear on the task:

Helping others succeed. This should always be your first priority at work. By helping others succeed, you help the company succeed, and yourself as well.

Learning. By expanding your knowledge base concerning your field you increase your value to the company. You also increase the chance that you will be able to contribute to (or be the source of) a breakthrough.

Which brings us to another equally beneficial use of your project time, thinking. In too many companies creative thinking is limited to brainstorming sessions. Brainstorming sessions just scratch the surface of the human potential for creative thought. Imagine what you might come up with if you had just an hour a day to ponder possibilities.

Lastly, another important use of project time is connecting. This may be with someone from another department, or a client company, or a company that your company has yet to do dealings with. The point is to connect with someone who represents a possibility. The possibility of sharing notes and being mutually benefited by comparing methods, forging the path to a corporate alliance, or just learning more about some aspect of your business.

Every step of the way this is your goal, bringing your talents to bear on the task of benefiting your company. Finding time to help others, to learn, to scheme and connect – therein lays the potential for excellence. By having a sense of urgency about your company's success, you assure your own.

GRAB YOUR GLOVES AND START PULLING:

The clock is ticking and nothing can stop it. Every moment wasted can never be reclaimed. Life is too precious to waste on trivialities. It's time to free yourself

from those worthless things we use to avoid facing
responsibility. It's time to pull the weeds:

"For my own sake,

for the sake of my family,

for the sake of everyone whose life I will touch,

I need to rip out the weeds in my life.

At home and at work

I will weed around the crop of a life well lived,

remembering that the momentary pain of removing

those intrusive roots

is a small price to pay for the harvest to come.

So I reach into the rich soil of my life,

and with trembling hands,

Lord help me,

I pull."

BRINGING IN THE HARVEST

"Let us not become weary in doing good,
for at the proper time we will reap a harvest if we do not give up."
Galatians 6:9 NIV

One year I decided to grow a field of oats. We really didn't have any need for oats; I think I grew it because of some fond memories of which growing oats was a part. The whole operation went smashingly, producing a beautiful field. I harvested it, put it in sacks, and stored it in the barn. Without a real plan of what to do with it, I just left it to winter in the barn.

The following spring I opened up the barn to find that the sacks had been eaten through by mice leaving an unsacked mound of oats. Not only that, the seeds on the surface had all sprouted, so the whole thing was light green and bushy. It looked like a one ton chia pet.

I have since learned my lesson, plant not what you enjoy planting, but what you want to harvest.

I now grow only what I want to harvest. My family gathers round as we enjoy the fresh produce our farm has produced, and I relish giving away bushels of tomatoes, potatoes, sweet corn and cucumbers. Then I make the rounds in my old Ford pickup truck. Feeling like Santa in his sleigh I hand out bushels of fresh produce to friends and neighbors.

All too often executives think of their harvest in terms of money, prestige or the pleasure of luxuries – to pile up like so much oats in the barn. Growing these crops is pleasurable, but in the end of little value compared to a loving family, close friends, good health, and the knowledge that you have really helped people.

The business world has another term for the harvest, "legacy." In the way legacy is usually described, they have it half right. Your legacy is not about money, prestige, power, or pleasures, and it is about having an impact on people in the marketplace. However, your legacy is so much more, it's everything you leave behind – nothing less than the imprint left by your whole life's work. Your legacy is the impact you have had on people at work, at home, and everywhere in between.

This is the essence of success: To have planted what you wanted to harvest, and to have harvested that which you planted. This may be a simple concept but it's a desperately needed one.

A legacy is shaped by three areas of action (or inaction) and three principles. The areas of action you are already acquainted with; setting life priorities, helping others, and having a sense of urgency. In this chapter I will introduce you to the three principles, integrity, integration, and purpose.

INTEGRITY

Gandhi emphasized,

"A person cannot do right in one department whilst attempting to do wrong in another department. Life is one indivisible whole."[18]

To have integrity is not just to have a set of moral guidelines, but also to act on them consistently in all

---

[18] Stephen R. Covey, Principle-Centered Leadership (New York: Summit Books, 1991), p. 323.

arenas of your life. Integrity makes decision-making simpler, though not necessarily easier. Following one set of morals and having one guiding star is considerably simpler; it means not having to separate business ethics from family ethics and not having a double standard to deal with and defend. Integrity, however, often makes decisions more emotionally difficult by requiring a personal loss to avoid a break with conscience.

I recently had a conversation with a long-standing client who was retiring. He made lots of money, had been touted as an outstanding leader, and has had two books written about him. One day we were musing and I asked, "Looking back, how do you define your life?"

He paused a few moments and said, "My life has been an accumulation of regrets."

I was stunned. He explained that 25 years ago he had lied in order to get a promotion. His lie not only led to his promotion, but to the firing of a friend of his. For years he has tried in vain to put that relationship together again but the former friend wanted nothing to do with him. He talked about lying and living a lie.

This man had a long-term marriage with no intimacy, a child who loves him only from a distance because he was never around when she was growing up. But he has power, money and all the toys he wants. Fortunately, even though he was haunted by his memories, he chose to pursue marriage counseling and is redoing what he can as a father and now grandfather. But the shadow of poor life choices lingers.

For this man, harvest time, a time of celebration, was darkened by a shadow of lost integrity. Preserve your harvest; apply yourself to a life of integrity.

INTEGRATION

For those aspiring to leadership, Max DePree says, "Leaders see a two-fold opportunity - to build a life and to build a career. And the fact is that people become leaders only by building both."[19]

Opportunity is a given in business and often overlooked in our personal lives. I often wonder how lives would change if we treated our subordinates with the same care as we treat our children, or our children with the same nurturing that we lavish upon our star employee. Think how people would flourish if we all gave our spouses the same respect as our bosses!

One of my clients is a guy who was considered to be a tough and hard-nosed person. When I was working with him, he was rather resistant. We had only worked together a couple of times when he said, "I find some value in this but let's move on

Finally I asked him a question, I said, "I don't know much about you. Do you have a family?"

"Well, I'm married... I have a daughter, too."

[19] Max DePree, Leadership Jazz (New York: Dell Publishing, 1992), p. 169.

"Tell me about your daughter."

He paused and he said, "Her name is Michelle, and she's five years old." Here's a guy who hadn't gotten married until his early 40s, he was now close to 50, and he had a 5-year-old daughter. When he started talking about Michelle he melted. He became warm and open and affable. He reached into his pocket and took out his wallet, showed me pictures of Michelle and told me about her learning how to walk. He was now teaching her how to ride a bicycle. Every night they read together. In that conversation, he became human.

I stopped him at one point and said, "Why can't you take that into the rest of your life?" He had maintained the myth that his purpose of being a good father needed to be estranged from everything else in his life. It's interesting to go into his office now. He has pictures of Michelle, he has pictures of his wife, and he has pictures of other people. When he goes into meetings, the first thing he does is to put Michelle's name at the top of his legal pad as a reminder to be more open and more human.

He said, "Out of the corner of my eye, I always see Michelle."

I've worked with some of his direct reports, and they've given me unsolicited feedback that this former curmudgeon has now added warmth and openness to his admirable leadership qualities.

"In fact, the process of becoming a leader is much the same as the process of becoming an integrated human being. For the leader, as for any integrated person, life itself is the career.'[20]

Integration is bringing the best of who you are at work home with you, and bringing the best of who you are at home to work. The result is a seamless life marked by continual self-improvement.

[20] Warren Bennis, On Becoming A Leader (New York: Addison-Wesley Publishing, 1989), p. 4.

The term purpose can be understood in many ways, allow me to clarify the way in which am I using it here: "Purpose" is having a goal which holds the promise of positively affecting people's lives. Having a sense of purpose, of mission, is essential if you wish to leave a lasting legacy.

One day I said to an executive at a client company, "What's your purpose in this company?"

He said, "To get the most out of these idiots that I can."

He was extremely disparaging of his employees. I asked him later about his family. I said, "What's your purpose in your family?"

"Bring home as much money as I can so they can do anything they want to." He was reactive and negative.

The CEO and other company executives went through a transformation process where their goals and behaviors became aligned. This person just never got it.

Later on this man went to the CEO and said, "I don't know what's going on around here, but I don't seem to fit in."

His boss said, "I think you're right."

The short term effect of his behavior was that he got fired, I'm sure you can imagine what the long term effects were.

Few of us would be so blunt but it is amazing how many people do not have any conception of their own purpose, only a vague sense of irritation regarding the issue.

Finding purpose is a highly individualized journey. There are no processes or tips I can recommend. Instead I offer you four examples, portraits if you will, of purpose:

❧ After I had worked with a client on some perfunctory aspects of leadership, I asked him, "What's your life purpose?" Unsure, he passed off the question.

A week later he called me at 3:00 a.m. and woke me up. He said, "Brekke, you're buggin' the hell out of me."

My sleepy response was, "What are you talking about?"

"I am in Venice with my wife. We're having brunch. It is a beautiful day and I started talking with my wife about life purpose. It became clear to me that my wife understands what her life purpose is and she has been living it for years. It is just as clear to me that even though I've attained all these things in my life, I still don't have a clear understanding of what my essential purpose is."

One day, months later, he said to me, "John, what I'd like you to help me do is to understand how to move people."

"What do you mean by that?"

He replied, "I have been at this company for almost 40 years. I've been highly effective. Here I am, chief honcho, but I don't think I have really helped people understand just how good they can be, what their vision might be, what their purpose is. I want to learn how to do that."

After we talked about it some more he realized he had hit upon his life purpose, "Now, I understand that the purpose for the rest of my life is to move people; to help them understand that they have a mission. I can be a motivational influence in helping them accomplish what they uniquely are here to do... and to be."

᠍ One of my clients went through a process to determine what their corporate mission was. One day, as we were working, I asked the chairman, "Sir, tell me about your company."

He described the company in terms of numbers, manufacturing facilities, their presence in 115 countries worldwide, the number of employees, and total annual revenue.

My response to that was essentially, "Big deal. You've described your company, but you haven't described what your purpose is." I helped him struggle for some time with the relationship between his corporation and life priorities.

Some time later I heard him in a discussion, when he was asked how he would define his organization he said, "This organization exists to meet some vital human needs." He gave examples of several products that met that criterion; one was important for people in cold climates and another was important for people who use technology.

Now that the chairman understood the significance of his company he was able to convey it to others in a manner that highlighted not the size of his company, but its importance to better human life.

People may respect size, but they are rarely motivated by it. In fact, the bigger the company the more an employee is aware of how little a contribution they make. Significance, however, can be highly motivating:

"We not only supply dairy products that are among the highest quality in the country, but we keep thousands of dairy farmers in business."

"Our hotdogs are so much a part of the American consciousness that they have become a symbol of childhood and America itself. And we offer the best tasting fat-free hot dog available."

"Our bikes are the safest made. Children's lives have no doubt been saved by our careful design."

"Our company makes the least painful insulin needle available, and I'm a part of that."

శ While at another company as I was waiting for an elevator I noticed a fellow with "Joe" embroidered on his shirt who was mopping the floor. I greeted him and he greeted me warmly with a big smile. I asked him a seemingly innocent question, "What's your job?"

He could have responded any number of ways, such as, "It's obvious what my job is, I'm cleaning up." He could have said that he was a janitor. He could have said that he was a custodian. He could have said that he was an engineer or given another title to describe people whose job it is to clean up. But he didn't.

He stopped and said to me, "My job is to keep these hallways clean and safe for people like you."

That answer blew me away. Here was a guy who clearly understood his role in the business environment. He didn't clean floors, he didn't empty wastebaskets, what he did was keep an environment clean and safe for people like me.

❧ The chairman of a multinational company, a year before he retired, said, "I finally figured out what being chairman of this company means. Being chairman is a means to an end; it is not an end in itself. It gives me access to people and access to power bases that can help me promote some issues that, important as my company is, are even more important."

This man is deeply invested in children's issues such as early childhood education, getting kids out of inner-city areas where children are having children, and helping kids identify their life priorities. He saw the vision of being an effective leader, going beyond simply being a leader for the moment. The world needs more leaders with his brand of vision and sense of life purpose. Seek your purpose, the world needs you.

BRINGING IN THE SHEAVES

Your harvest is in your hands, all the work in the world cannot compensate for a lack of integration, integrity, and purpose. Make a stand, right now:

"I will bring the best of myself to all areas of my life,

I will live a life of simple integrity despite the cost,

and I will strive to understand my life

in terms of purpose,

always keeping in mind that

the most precious thing in life

is the chance to influence another's."

EPILOGUE

In this book I have attempted to redefine for you the nature of success, effective leadership, and life balance. If you have read carefully you may have noticed that each of these contains a profound irony:

In order to best succeed at work –

it cannot be your first priority.

By serving others –

you help yourself.

By having a sense of urgency –

you have more time to enjoy life.

Developing as a leader and building a career and life are ultimately unfinished projects, they are works in progress. We are forever plowing, planting, and weeding. We are also forever harvesting the fruits of our efforts.

So take control, roll up your sleeves and get your hands dirty. The fields are wide and the soil rich, just waiting for you to break the ground.

And so you go, seed sack over your shoulder, spreading seeds on the freshly plowed earth. You carefully weed the rows and nervously you wait.

Will you achieve success? Will your live to see your grandchildren? Can your marriage be a source of joy? Will your children love you when they are grown? Will all your patience and hard work really pay off?

Then, one misty morning, a thousand tender shoots....

SUGGESTED READING

Arbinger Institute, *Leadership And Self Deception*, Berrett-Koehler Publishers (2000).

Bennis, Warren, *On Becoming A Leader*, Addison-Wesley Publishing Company (1989).

Buckingham, Marcus & Curt Coffman, *First, Break All The Rules*, Simon & Schuster (1999).

Buckingham, Marcus & Curt Coffman, *Now, Discover Your Strengths*, The Free Press (2001).

Collins, Jim, *Good To Great*, HarperCollins*Publishers* (2001).

DePree, Max, *Leadership Is An Art*, Dell Publishing (1989).

George, Bill, *Authentic Leadership: Rediscovering The Secrets To Creating Lasting Value*, Jossey-Bass (2003).

Gladwell, Malcolm, *The Tipping Point: How Little Things Can Make A Big Difference*, Little, Brown & Company (2000).

Goleman, Daniel, *Working With Emotional Intelligence*, Dell Publishing (1998).

Jaworski, Joseph, *Synchronicity: The Inner Path Of Leadership*, Berrett-Koehler Publishers (1996).

Kushner, Harold, *Living A Life That Matters*, First Anchor Books (2001).

Lencioni, Patrick, *The Four Obsessions Of An Extraordinary Executive,* Jossey-Bass (2000).

McNally, David, *Even Eagles Need A Push: Learning To Soar In A Changing World,* Dell Publishing (1990).

ABOUT THE AUTHORS

 John L. Brekke is one of the nation's veteran executive coaches. He spent much of his childhood growing up on a farm in Northern Minnesota, and started his first business repairing clocks at age 14. He has been a television and radio broadcaster, a high school and college teacher and a college dean. His entrepreneurial career includes owning a real estate agency and a publishing company. He got his start studying leadership as the recipient of a Kellogg Foundation Leadership grant, and now owns his own executive consulting company.

For the past 27 years, John has been an executive coach with a focus on leadership skills. He has worked with senior executives of many Fortune 500 companies, including 3M, Honeywell, Pfizer, Wells Fargo, Piper Jaffray, General Growth Properties, Case (CNH), Cigna, United Health Group, and Faegre & Benson. He is a sought-after speaker on highly provocative leadership topics.

He returns to tend his small farm in rural Minnesota.

 David L. Brekke is John's younger son and partner in the business. As Senior Vice President, David has graced Brekke Consulting with his skills as a psychometrician, coach, strategic analyst and writer.

BREKKE CONSULTING, INC.

*Counsel and Coaching for
Executives*

FURTHER INFORMATION ABOUT THE WORK OF
BREKKE CONSULTING, INC.
CAN BE OBTAINED BY LOGGING ON TO
WWW.BREKKECONSULTING.COM

IF YOU ARE INTERESTED IN THE SPEAKING WORK OF
JOHN BREKKE PLEASE LOG ON TO
WWW.JOHNLBREKKE.COM